PRINCEWILL LAGANG

Love Letters from God: Daily Devotions for Couples

First published by PRINCEWILL LAGANG 2023

Copyright © 2023 by Princewill Lagang

All rights reserved. No part of this publication may be reproduced, stored or transmitted in any form or by any means, electronic, mechanical, photocopying, recording, scanning, or otherwise without written permission from the publisher. It is illegal to copy this book, post it to a website, or distribute it by any other means without permission.

Princewill Lagang asserts the moral right to be identified as the author of this work.

First edition

This book was professionally typeset on Reedsy.
Find out more at reedsy.com

Contents

1	A Journey of Love and Faith	1
2	The Language of Love	4
3	The Gratitude of Love	7
4	The Healing Power of Forgiveness	10
5	The Gentle Strength of Patience	13
6	The Radiance of Hope	16
7	The Enduring Joy of Love	19
8	The Steadfast Anchor of Commitment	22
9	The Grace of Love	25
10	Commitment to Self-Growth	28
11	The Wisdom of Togetherness	31
12	The Eternal Bond of Love	34

1

A Journey of Love and Faith

Title: Love Letters from God: Daily Devotions for Couples

Introduction

In the quiet embrace of the early morning, as the sun's gentle rays tiptoe through your window, you find yourself wrapped in the warmth of a new day. It's a brand new chapter in the beautiful love story you share with your partner. The sweet scent of fresh coffee wafts through the air as you sit together, eyes still heavy with sleep, but hearts already light with anticipation.

Love is an incredible force, transcending time, space, and circumstance. It's a gift, a privilege, and a responsibility. This is the essence of "Love Letters from God: Daily Devotions for Couples." Within these pages, you'll embark on a year-long journey, a daily devotion designed to strengthen the bond between you and your partner, renew your faith, and deepen your love.

Chapter 1: A Journey of Love and Faith

In this first chapter, we set the stage for the adventure that lies ahead. We explore the foundations of love, faith, and how these two powerful forces intersect to form the bedrock of a thriving relationship. As you dive into this chapter, take a moment to reflect on your own love story—the moments that brought you together, the trials you've faced, and the growth you've experienced as a couple.

Section 1: Love as a Divine Gift

Love is a gift from a higher power, something that transcends our understanding, and is often referred to as a divine force. In this section, we discuss the idea that love is a sacred, otherworldly emotion that flows from a source beyond ourselves. It's a force that binds us together, encouraging us to care, nurture, and support one another.

Section 2: Faith as the Bridge

Faith, in the context of this journey, represents more than religious belief. It is the unwavering trust in the love you share, the belief in a better tomorrow, and the understanding that your relationship is a sacred covenant. We explore the role of faith as a bridge connecting two hearts, allowing love to flow freely and abundantly.

Section 3: Building a Strong Foundation

To withstand the challenges of life and the tests of time, every couple needs a solid foundation. We'll delve into the practical aspects of building this foundation, including open communication, mutual respect, and shared values. As you read, consider how you can implement these principles in your own relationship.

Section 4: Daily Devotions as a Ritual

The heart of this book lies in the daily devotions—short readings, prayers, and reflections designed to be shared with your partner. These devotions provide a daily pause, a sacred moment for you and your loved one to connect, reflect, and grow. We will discuss the importance of integrating this daily practice into your lives.

Closing Thoughts

As you embark on this journey through "Love Letters from God: Daily Devotions for Couples," remember that love is a living, breathing entity. It requires care, attention, and nurturing to thrive. Your love story is a reflection of divine love, and together, you can make it a masterpiece.

Each day, as you open these pages, let the words, prayers, and reflections be your guide. They are love letters from God, reminding you that love and faith are the threads that weave the tapestry of your lives together. The journey begins with this chapter, but the story is yours to write.

May you find inspiration and strength within these pages, as you walk hand in hand on the path of love and faith, strengthening the bond between you and your beloved, and discovering the ever-present, ever-renewing love of God that surrounds you.

2

The Language of Love

Title: Love Letters from God: Daily Devotions for Couples

Introduction

In Chapter 1, you embarked on a journey to explore the profound connection between love and faith, establishing a foundation for the devotion and commitment you share with your partner. As we move forward into Chapter 2 of "Love Letters from God: Daily Devotions for Couples," we delve deeper into the art of communication within a loving relationship. Much like a letter composed from the heart, the language of love is a skill that must be honed and cultivated.

Chapter 2: The Language of Love

In this chapter, you'll learn how to express love, appreciation, and understanding through a language that transcends spoken words. We'll discuss the myriad ways in which you can communicate your affection, fostering a deeper connection with your partner.

Section 1: The Power of Non-Verbal Communication

Communication is not solely about the words you speak. It also encompasses the silent language of gestures, touch, and shared experiences. This section encourages you to explore the power of non-verbal communication in your relationship. Through these subtle yet significant cues, you can express your love and affection without saying a word.

Section 2: The Art of Listening

Effective communication is a two-way street. It's not just about what you say but also about how well you listen. We will discuss active listening techniques that can strengthen your connection, deepen your understanding of each other, and make your partner feel truly heard and valued.

Section 3: Love Languages

Every person has their unique way of both expressing and receiving love. In this section, you'll explore the concept of love languages. By understanding your partner's primary love language, you can tailor your expressions of love to be more meaningful and fulfilling for them. We'll delve into the five love languages—words of affirmation, acts of service, receiving gifts, quality time, and physical touch—and how to identify which one resonates most with your partner.

Section 4: Conflict Resolution

Conflict is an inevitable part of any relationship. But, as we discuss in this section, it can be an opportunity for growth and deeper understanding. Learn healthy conflict resolution techniques that will help you navigate disagreements with love and respect, ultimately bringing you closer rather than driving you apart.

Section 5: The Love Letter Ritual

In each section of this book, we emphasize the importance of the daily devotional practice. In this section, you will learn how to incorporate the language of love into your daily devotionals. Explore ways to express your love for your partner through these daily rituals, strengthening your bond and fostering deeper connection.

Closing Thoughts

As you immerse yourself in the language of love and communication, remember that each day is an opportunity to strengthen your connection with your partner. The words, actions, and gestures you choose can either nourish your love or let it wither. With the insights gained in this chapter, you're now better equipped to cultivate a thriving, loving relationship.

In Chapter 3, we will explore the significance of gratitude in your journey of love and faith. Until then, may your words and deeds reflect the beauty of your love, creating a lasting symphony of affection between you and your beloved.

3

The Gratitude of Love

Title: Love Letters from God: Daily Devotions for Couples

Introduction

As you continue your journey through "Love Letters from God: Daily Devotions for Couples," you've already explored the foundations of love and faith, delved into the language of love, and learned how to express your affection for your partner. Now, in Chapter 3, we turn our focus to the profound and transformative power of gratitude within your relationship.

Chapter 3: The Gratitude of Love

Gratitude is a magnetic force that draws love closer and deeper. It's a transformative attitude that can shift your perspective and strengthen the bond between you and your partner. In this chapter, you will learn to embrace gratitude as an essential component of your journey through love and faith.

Section 1: The Power of Gratitude

Gratitude is more than simply saying "thank you." It is a heartwarming acknowledgment of the blessings and love that grace your life daily. In this section, we'll explore the significance of gratitude in love and the profound impact it can have on your relationship.

Section 2: Recognizing the Blessings

It's easy to take the blessings in our lives for granted. In this section, you'll learn how to recognize and appreciate the everyday blessings that both you and your partner bring into each other's lives. From the little gestures to the profound moments, we'll discuss how gratitude can illuminate the beauty in even the smallest acts of love.

Section 3: The Ripple Effect of Gratitude

Gratitude has a ripple effect—it not only nourishes your relationship but also extends its warmth to the world around you. We'll explore how expressing gratitude for your partner can inspire a more generous, compassionate, and loving approach to others and the world at large.

Section 4: Gratitude in Daily Devotion

In this section, we'll discuss how to incorporate gratitude into your daily devotionals. Expressing thankfulness and appreciation for each other and for the love you share can deepen your connection, reinforce your faith, and remind you of the divine presence in your lives.

Section 5: Acts of Love through Gratitude

Gratitude is not just about words; it's also about actions. We'll delve into the meaningful acts of love that can express your gratitude and deepen your bond. Whether it's a surprise gesture, a loving note, or a simple act of service, these actions will reflect the gratitude you feel for your partner.

Closing Thoughts

Gratitude is the thread that weaves love and faith together. As you immerse yourself in this chapter, reflect on the blessings that your partner brings into your life and how the practice of gratitude can enhance your love. Every day is an opportunity to acknowledge the divine love that surrounds you, and through your gratitude, you can make your relationship a living testament to the love of God.

In Chapter 4, we will explore the importance of forgiveness and how it can be a profound act of love within your relationship. Until then, may gratitude fill your hearts, deepen your connection, and shine a light on the path of love and faith that you walk together.

4

The Healing Power of Forgiveness

Title: Love Letters from God: Daily Devotions for Couples

Introduction

As you've journeyed through the pages of "Love Letters from God: Daily Devotions for Couples," you've explored the foundations of love and faith, the language of love, and the transformative power of gratitude within your relationship. Now, in Chapter 4, we delve into the profound and healing power of forgiveness—a fundamental aspect of maintaining a loving and lasting partnership.

Chapter 4: The Healing Power of Forgiveness

Forgiveness is an essential tool in the kit of a thriving relationship. It holds the power to mend wounds, to release burdens, and to deepen your love and faith. In this chapter, you'll explore the significance of forgiveness in love and learn how to incorporate it into your daily devotions.

Section 1: The Heart's Burden

Every relationship experiences its share of missteps, misunderstandings, and hurtful moments. This section addresses the emotional weight carried by these experiences and the importance of unburdening your heart through forgiveness.

Section 2: The Act of Forgiveness

Forgiveness is not a one-time event but a continuous process. We'll discuss the steps involved in the act of forgiveness, emphasizing the need for understanding, empathy, and genuine reconciliation.

Section 3: Forgiving Ourselves

Sometimes, we must forgive ourselves for our own mistakes and shortcomings. We'll explore the importance of self-forgiveness and how it's closely tied to your ability to forgive others.

Section 4: Rebuilding Trust

Forgiveness is a crucial step in rebuilding trust in a relationship. We'll discuss how trust can be restored through open communication, consistency, and a shared commitment to a renewed and stronger bond.

Section 5: Forgiveness in Daily Devotion

Forgiveness can be an integral part of your daily devotional practice. We'll explore how you can incorporate forgiveness into your daily readings and prayers, allowing this act of love to strengthen your bond and deepen your faith.

Closing Thoughts

Forgiveness is an act of love that requires courage and empathy. It's a testament to the strength of your love, your faith in one another, and your commitment to the growth and well-being of your relationship. As you immerse yourself in this chapter, consider the opportunities for forgiveness that may exist in your partnership and the healing power it can unleash.

In Chapter 5, we will explore the role of patience in nurturing your love and faith. Until then, may forgiveness guide your hearts towards greater understanding, compassion, and a deepening connection in the sacred journey of love.

5

The Gentle Strength of Patience

Title: Love Letters from God: Daily Devotions for Couples

Introduction

In your journey through "Love Letters from God: Daily Devotions for Couples," you've explored the foundations of love and faith, the language of love, the transformative power of gratitude, and the profound healing potential of forgiveness. Now, in Chapter 5, we delve into the gentle yet profound strength of patience in nurturing love and faith.

Chapter 5: The Gentle Strength of Patience

Patience is a virtue that can be a soothing balm in the midst of life's trials and tribulations. It allows love to blossom and faith to deepen. In this chapter, you will learn how patience can become a cornerstone of your relationship.

Section 1: The Role of Patience

Patience is not merely the ability to wait; it is the capacity to maintain a positive attitude during the waiting period. We discuss the role of patience in your relationship, highlighting its power to calm turbulent waters, temper reactions, and guide your journey with a steadying hand.

Section 2: Navigating Challenges

Every relationship faces challenges. In this section, we delve into how patience can be your guiding light when confronting difficulties. It encourages you to remain calm, composed, and unwavering in your faith that you and your partner can overcome whatever comes your way.

Section 3: Communication and Understanding

Patience plays a pivotal role in effective communication. We explore how patience can enhance understanding between you and your partner, allowing you to truly listen, empathize, and bridge any gaps in your relationship.

Section 4: The Growth of Love

Patience is the soil in which love can flourish. We discuss how the patient nurturing of love can lead to deeper, more profound connections over time, helping your relationship to mature and strengthen.

Section 5: Patience in Daily Devotion

Incorporating patience into your daily devotional practice can be transformative. We'll explore how waiting, listening, and giving space for divine guidance can deepen your faith and nurture your love in this section.

Closing Thoughts

Patience is a precious gift that you can give to your relationship, your partner, and yourself. It allows your love to blossom and your faith to grow stronger with each passing day. As you immerse yourself in this chapter, consider the ways in which patience can be a guiding force in your journey through love and faith.

In Chapter 6, we will explore the power of hope in your relationship and how it can be a beacon of light, even in the darkest of times. Until then, may the gentle strength of patience guide your hearts towards deeper understanding, compassion, and a more profound connection on the sacred path of love.

6

The Radiance of Hope

Title: Love Letters from God: Daily Devotions for Couples

Introduction

In your journey through "Love Letters from God: Daily Devotions for Couples," you've explored the foundations of love and faith, the language of love, the transformative power of gratitude, the profound healing potential of forgiveness, and the gentle strength of patience. Now, in Chapter 6, we delve into the radiant power of hope in nurturing love and faith, especially during challenging times.

Chapter 6: The Radiance of Hope

Hope is the gentle whisper in the darkest hours, the flicker of light in the bleakest of moments. It is the driving force that propels you forward, illuminating the path of love and faith. In this chapter, you will learn how hope can be your guiding star, especially when faced with adversity.

Section 1: The Role of Hope

Hope is more than wishful thinking; it is a belief in the possibility of a better future. We discuss the central role of hope in your relationship, especially in times of uncertainty and adversity, and how it can serve as an anchor for your love and faith.

Section 2: Navigating Challenges

Challenges are an inevitable part of life and relationships. This section explores how hope can inspire resilience, courage, and a positive outlook, even in the face of the most formidable challenges.

Section 3: Building a Vision

Hope is the foundation on which dreams are built. We discuss how hope can inspire you to create a vision for your shared future, helping you to set and pursue shared goals that strengthen your connection.

Section 4: Love's Resilience

Hope is the sustenance of love during difficult times. We delve into how hope can help you and your partner weather storms, emerging from challenges with a deeper love and unwavering faith in your relationship.

Section 5: Hope in Daily Devotion

Incorporating hope into your daily devotional practice can be a beacon of light during your journey. We'll explore how daily reflections on hope can deepen your faith and brighten the path of love, even in the darkest of times.

Closing Thoughts

Hope is the fire that fuels your love and faith. It's the belief in the love you share, the strength of your bond, and the bright future that awaits you. As you immerse yourself in this chapter, consider the ways in which hope can be a radiant force in your journey through love and faith, particularly when you encounter adversity.

In Chapter 7, we will explore the enduring importance of joy and how it can be a source of strength and connection in your relationship. Until then, may the radiance of hope light your way, fortify your bond, and guide your hearts on the sacred path of love.

7

The Enduring Joy of Love

Title: Love Letters from God: Daily Devotions for Couples

Introduction

In your journey through "Love Letters from God: Daily Devotions for Couples," you've explored the foundations of love and faith, the language of love, the transformative power of gratitude, the profound healing potential of forgiveness, the gentle strength of patience, and the radiant power of hope. Now, in Chapter 7, we delve into the enduring joy that love can bring and how it can be a source of strength and connection in your relationship.

Chapter 7: The Enduring Joy of Love

Joy is a radiant light that shines even in the ordinary moments of life. It is the laughter in shared stories, the delight in each other's company, and the deep-seated happiness that comes from loving and being loved. In this chapter, you will explore the significance of joy in nurturing love and faith.

Section 1: The Role of Joy

Joy is more than just happiness; it is a state of being that transcends circumstances. We discuss the central role of joy in your relationship, as it brings warmth, positivity, and light to your love and faith.

Section 2: Cultivating Shared Experiences

Joy often arises from shared experiences. This section explores the power of creating memorable moments together, and how they can be a wellspring of joy that deepens your connection.

Section 3: Fostering Laughter

Laughter is the music of joy. We delve into how humor and playfulness can infuse your relationship with laughter, lightening your burdens and deepening your bond.

Section 4: Savoring the Present

Joy is often found in the present moment. We discuss how mindfulness and gratitude can help you and your partner appreciate the beauty in everyday life, thereby enhancing your love and faith.

Section 5: Joy in Daily Devotion

Incorporating joy into your daily devotional practice can infuse your journey with positivity and connection. We'll explore how daily reflections on joy can deepen your faith and remind you of the happiness that comes from loving and being loved.

Closing Thoughts

Joy is the enduring undercurrent of love. It's the light that brightens your path, the laughter that fills your hearts, and the happiness that emanates from your bond. As you immerse yourself in this chapter, consider the ways in which joy can be a source of strength, positivity, and connection in your journey through love and faith.

In Chapter 8, we will explore the importance of commitment in your relationship and how it can be a steadfast anchor during the ebbs and flows of life. Until then, may the enduring joy of love light your way, deepen your bond, and guide your hearts on the sacred path of love.

8

The Steadfast Anchor of Commitment

Title: Love Letters from God: Daily Devotions for Couples

Introduction

In your journey through "Love Letters from God: Daily Devotions for Couples," you've explored the foundations of love and faith, the language of love, the transformative power of gratitude, the profound healing potential of forgiveness, the gentle strength of patience, the radiant power of hope, and the enduring joy of love. Now, in Chapter 8, we delve into the unwavering strength of commitment within your relationship.

Chapter 8: The Steadfast Anchor of Commitment

Commitment is the rock upon which the foundation of lasting love is built. It is the unyielding pledge to stand by one another, to nurture and protect your love and faith through the storms and sunshine of life. In this chapter, you will learn how commitment can be your steady anchor through all the ebbs and flows.

Section 1: The Role of Commitment

THE STEADFAST ANCHOR OF COMMITMENT

Commitment is more than mere words; it is a profound promise to be there for one another. We discuss the central role of commitment in your relationship, emphasizing how it can be the unwavering anchor that keeps you grounded through all seasons of life.

Section 2: Weathering Life's Storms

Every relationship faces storms and challenges. In this section, we explore how commitment can be your strength during tough times. It encourages you to stand by your partner's side, support one another, and find solutions together.

Section 3: Nurturing Your Love

Commitment requires effort and care. We delve into the ways you can continually nurture your love, reinforcing your connection and your shared commitment to each other.

Section 4: Growing Together

Commitment is not static; it evolves and deepens with time. We discuss how commitment can help you and your partner grow together, building a love that is ever more profound and lasting.

Section 5: Commitment in Daily Devotion

Incorporating commitment into your daily devotional practice can remind you of the strength of your bond. We'll explore how daily reflections on commitment can deepen your faith and reaffirm your dedication to each other.

Closing Thoughts

Commitment is the unwavering anchor of love. It is the promise that you and your partner will stand together, through all the highs and lows of life. As you immerse yourself in this chapter, consider the ways in which commitment can be a steadfast anchor during the ebbs and flows of your journey through love and faith.

In Chapter 9, we will explore the importance of grace and how it can be a source of compassion, forgiveness, and strength within your relationship. Until then, may the steadfast anchor of commitment guide your hearts and reinforce your bond on the sacred path of love.

9

The Grace of Love

Title: Love Letters from God: Daily Devotions for Couples

Introduction

In your journey through "Love Letters from God: Daily Devotions for Couples," you've explored the foundations of love and faith, the language of love, the transformative power of gratitude, the profound healing potential of forgiveness, the gentle strength of patience, the radiant power of hope, the enduring joy of love, and the steadfast anchor of commitment. Now, in Chapter 9, we delve into the grace of love and how it can be a wellspring of compassion, forgiveness, and strength within your relationship.

Chapter 9: The Grace of Love

Grace is the unmerited favor bestowed upon us, a divine gift that flows through our lives, especially in our relationships. It is the compassion, forgiveness, and understanding that we extend to one another, even in the face of imperfections. In this chapter, you will learn how grace can be a wellspring of love, compassion, and strength in your daily devotion.

Section 1: The Role of Grace

Grace is more than an act of kindness; it is an embodiment of love. We discuss the central role of grace in your relationship, highlighting how it can be the foundation of compassion and understanding for both you and your partner.

Section 2: Extending Compassion

Compassion is a vital aspect of grace. In this section, we explore the ways in which compassion can strengthen your relationship, allowing you to understand and support one another in times of need.

Section 3: Forgiveness as Grace

Forgiveness is a significant part of grace. We delve into the profound act of forgiving one another, even when it's difficult, and how it can heal wounds and deepen your love and faith.

Section 4: Cultivating Understanding

Grace fosters understanding. We discuss how grace can help you and your partner gain insights into each other's perspectives, encouraging empathy and a deeper connection.

Section 5: Grace in Daily Devotion

Incorporating grace into your daily devotional practice can transform your journey. We'll explore how daily reflections on grace can deepen your faith and remind you of the beauty of extending love, compassion, and forgiveness.

Closing Thoughts

Grace is the unending flow of love. It is the compassion, forgiveness, and understanding that we extend to one another. As you immerse yourself in this chapter, consider the ways in which grace can be a wellspring of love, compassion, and strength in your journey through love and faith.

In Chapter 10, we will explore the significance of commitment to self-growth within your relationship, and how it can be a source of personal and collective transformation. Until then, may the grace of love guide your hearts and deepen your bond on the sacred path of love.

10

Commitment to Self-Growth

Title: Love Letters from God: Daily Devotions for Couples

Introduction

As you near the conclusion of your journey through "Love Letters from God: Daily Devotions for Couples," you've explored the foundations of love and faith, the language of love, the transformative power of gratitude, the profound healing potential of forgiveness, the gentle strength of patience, the radiant power of hope, the enduring joy of love, the steadfast anchor of commitment, and the grace of love. Now, in Chapter 10, we delve into the significance of commitment to self-growth within your relationship and how it can be a source of personal and collective transformation.

Chapter 10: Commitment to Self-Growth

The commitment to self-growth is a promise to continually evolve, both individually and as a couple. It is the acknowledgment that your relationship is a journey of self-discovery, learning, and transformation. In this chapter, you will learn how commitment to self-growth can be a catalyst for personal and collective growth within your relationship.

COMMITMENT TO SELF-GROWTH

Section 1: The Role of Self-Growth

Self-growth is a fundamental aspect of a thriving relationship. We discuss the central role of commitment to self-growth in your journey, emphasizing how it can contribute to your individual well-being and the health of your partnership.

Section 2: Embracing Change

Change is a natural part of life. In this section, we explore how commitment to self-growth involves embracing change, both in yourself and in your partner, and how it can lead to a deeper, more harmonious connection.

Section 3: Learning Together

Self-growth often involves learning and personal development. We delve into how learning together, whether through shared experiences, self-improvement, or acquiring new skills, can strengthen your bond and support each other's growth.

Section 4: Reflection and Self-Discovery

Self-growth is a journey of reflection and self-discovery. We discuss how taking time for self-reflection and understanding your own needs and desires can contribute to your growth as a person and as a couple.

Section 5: Self-Growth in Daily Devotion

Incorporating commitment to self-growth into your daily devotional practice can inspire personal and collective transformation. We'll explore how daily reflections on self-growth can deepen your faith and commitment to evolving together.

Closing Thoughts

The commitment to self-growth is a journey that never truly ends. It's the acknowledgment that both you and your partner will continually evolve, learn, and grow. As you immerse yourself in this chapter, consider the ways in which commitment to self-growth can be a source of personal and collective transformation within your journey through love and faith.

As you complete your journey in this book, remember that your love story is a living testament to the divine love that surrounds you. May your commitment to self-growth guide your hearts towards personal and collective transformation, reinforcing the bond that you share on the sacred path of love.

11

The Wisdom of Togetherness

Title: Love Letters from God: Daily Devotions for Couples

Introduction

As you approach the culmination of your journey through "Love Letters from God: Daily Devotions for Couples," you have explored various facets of love and faith, including gratitude, forgiveness, patience, hope, joy, commitment, grace, and the commitment to self-growth. In Chapter 11, we delve into the wisdom of togetherness, celebrating the rich experiences and lessons learned as a couple.

Chapter 11: The Wisdom of Togetherness

Togetherness is a source of wisdom that comes from shared experiences, challenges, and celebrations. It is the embodiment of the phrase, "two heads are better than one." In this chapter, you will reflect on the wisdom acquired through your shared journey and how it has deepened your love and faith.

Section 1: The Role of Togetherness

Togetherness forms the crucible in which your relationship is shaped and molded. We discuss the central role of togetherness in your journey, emphasizing how the wisdom acquired as a couple can guide your decisions and strengthen your bond.

Section 2: Shared Experiences

Your shared experiences provide the foundation for your wisdom. In this section, we explore how the trials and triumphs you've faced together have enriched your relationship and provided valuable insights for the journey ahead.

Section 3: Lessons from Challenges

Challenges have been a part of your journey. We delve into how these challenges have provided valuable life lessons that have deepened your wisdom and, in turn, your love and faith.

Section 4: Celebrating Achievements

Your achievements, whether big or small, have been a testament to your perseverance and the wisdom you've acquired as a couple. We discuss how celebrating your achievements can reinforce your bond and inspire continued growth.

Section 5: Togetherness in Daily Devotion

Incorporating the wisdom of togetherness into your daily devotional practice can remind you of the value of shared experiences and growth. We'll explore how daily reflections on togetherness can deepen your faith and your commitment to continue growing together.

Closing Thoughts

THE WISDOM OF TOGETHERNESS

The wisdom of togetherness is a gift that continues to unfold as your journey progresses. It's the realization that, together, you are stronger and wiser. As you conclude your journey in this book, reflect on the profound wisdom you've gained as a couple and how it has deepened your love and faith.

May the wisdom of togetherness guide your hearts towards greater understanding, compassion, and a deeper connection on the sacred path of love.

12

The Eternal Bond of Love

Title: Love Letters from God: Daily Devotions for Couples

Introduction

As you approach the conclusion of your journey through "Love Letters from God: Daily Devotions for Couples," you've explored numerous facets of love and faith, including gratitude, forgiveness, patience, hope, joy, commitment, grace, the commitment to self-growth, the wisdom of togetherness, and the lessons you've learned as a couple. In Chapter 12, we delve into the concept of the eternal bond of love, celebrating the enduring and timeless nature of your connection.

Chapter 12: The Eternal Bond of Love

The bond of love, once forged, is not subject to the constraints of time and space. It transcends the boundaries of this earthly existence, persisting as a testament to the divine nature of love. In this chapter, you will reflect on the eternal quality of your love and faith, and how it remains a source of strength and inspiration.

Section 1: The Timeless Nature of Love

Love is not limited by time; it has the power to endure beyond the years. We discuss the timeless nature of love and how it continues to grow and deepen, even as life unfolds.

Section 2: Love's Legacy

Your love story creates a lasting legacy. In this section, we explore how the love you share serves as a beacon of hope and inspiration for others, leaving an indelible mark on the world.

Section 3: The Divine Connection

Love is often described as a divine force. We delve into how this divine connection, nurtured by faith, continues to be a source of strength and guidance, regardless of the trials and tribulations you face.

Section 4: Reflecting on Your Journey

Take time to reflect on the journey you've embarked upon as a couple. We'll discuss the moments that have shaped your love and faith and how they have contributed to the eternal nature of your bond.

Section 5: Embracing the Future

As you conclude this journey, consider the path that lies ahead. We discuss how the eternal bond of love can guide your hearts toward a future filled with shared dreams, continued growth, and unwavering commitment.

Closing Thoughts

The eternal bond of love is a gift that will remain with you throughout your journey. It is a reminder of the timeless nature of love and faith. As you conclude this chapter and your journey in this book, remember that your love story is an enduring testament to the love that surrounds you.

May the eternal bond of love continue to deepen your connection, inspire your growth, and serve as a testament to the divine love that envelops you on the sacred path of love.

Book Summary: "Love Letters from God: Daily Devotions for Couples"

"Love Letters from God: Daily Devotions for Couples" is a heartfelt and spiritually enriching guide designed to nourish the love and faith of couples on their journey together. This book, consisting of 12 chapters, explores a wide range of themes and emotions, all underpinned by the belief in the divine presence of love.

Each chapter delves into a unique aspect of love, highlighting its transformative power and the profound influence it has on the faith and commitment between couples. The book doesn't just offer practical advice but also encourages couples to deepen their understanding of each other and their connection to a higher spiritual purpose.

Here is a brief summary of each chapter:

1. Chapter 1: Love's Foundation
   - Exploring the connection between love and faith as the cornerstone of a strong relationship.

2. Chapter 2: The Language of Love
   - Delving into the art of communication in a loving relationship, emphasizing the importance of words and actions.

3. Chapter 3: The Gratitude of Love

- Discussing the transformative power of gratitude in strengthening the bond between couples.

4. Chapter 4: The Healing Power of Forgiveness
   - Exploring the profound act of forgiveness and its role in conflict resolution and growth.

5. Chapter 5: The Gentle Strength of Patience
   - Delving into the importance of patience in nurturing love, and how it can be a soothing balm in challenging times.

6. Chapter 6: The Radiance of Hope
   - Highlighting the significance of hope in maintaining a positive outlook even in the face of adversity.

7. Chapter 7: The Enduring Joy of Love
   - Discussing the role of joy in deepening connections and bringing happiness into everyday life.

8. Chapter 8: The Steadfast Anchor of Commitment
   - Exploring the importance of commitment as an unwavering promise of support and love.

9. Chapter 9: The Grace of Love
   - Focusing on compassion, forgiveness, and understanding as expressions of love within a relationship.

10. Chapter 10: Commitment to Self-Growth
    - Discussing the commitment to personal and collective growth within a relationship.

11. Chapter 11: The Wisdom of Togetherness
    - Exploring the wisdom gained through shared experiences, challenges,

and achievements as a couple.

12. Chapter 12: The Eternal Bond of Love
   - Celebrating the enduring and timeless nature of love and its divine connection.

"Love Letters from God: Daily Devotions for Couples" is not only a guide to strengthening your relationship but also a reminder of the divine presence of love in your journey. It encourages couples to reflect on their connection, deepen their faith, and continue to grow together. With daily devotionals and reflections, this book serves as a testament to the enduring and transformative power of love in the lives of couples who seek to walk the sacred path of love and faith.

www.ingramcontent.com/pod-product-compliance
Lightning Source LLC
LaVergne TN
LVHW010439070526
838199LV00066B/6093